CW00486230

Blockchain Fundamentals

Here's How the Technology Behind Bitcoin, Ethereum and Other Cryptocurrencies Is Transforming the World

By

Joe Bears

Table of Contents

Introduction

The Blockchain is a technology that allows the transfer of data in a completely secure way thanks to a very sophisticated encryption. It is often compared to a company's ledger where all the inflows and outflows of money are recorded. Of course, in this case, we would be talking about a digital ledger of events.

Speaking of Blockchain means speaking about the technology (the information encoding system) behind Bitcoin. However, its function goes beyond that. It also serves to create other cryptocurrencies that are based on the same principles, but have other properties (policy, algorithm, etc.).

The Blockchain contributes to a great novelty. And it is that this transfer does not need an intermediary to check and approve the information, but it is distributed among several independent nodes that register and validate it. Therefore, the information cannot be deleted once it is introduced, only new records can be added. Moreover, it will not be legitimized unless the majority of them agree to do so. The latter is considered mission impossible.

Chapter 1: Developing the Knowledge Base

The method is designed to timestamp data files so that they cannot be backdated or tempered. The goal of Blockchain is to eliminate the need for a central server to solve the problem of duplicate records. The Blockchain is used to securely move objects such as currency, land, contracts, and other information without the need for a third-party broker such as a bank or government.

It is very difficult to alter data after it has been stored in a Blockchain. The Blockchain is a computer program. Blockchains, on the other hand, do not function without the Internet. It's also known as meta-technology, and it has an effect on other systems. It is made up of many components, including a database, a software program, and several related computers. The term is often used to refer to the Bitcoin or Ethereum Blockchains, and at other times it refers to other digital currencies or tokens. However, the majority of them are discussing distributed ledger technology.

What Blockchain Is Not

- The digital token is Bitcoin, and the Blockchain is the registry that keeps records about who holds the digital tokens.
- Bitcoin cannot exist without Blockchain, but Blockchain does exist without Bitcoin.
- Blockchain is not the same as Bitcoin, but it is also the infrastructure that makes Bitcoin possible.

Blockchain Architecture

Now, let's look at the Blockchain framework and its different components in this Blockchain Technology tutorial:

What is a Block?

A Blockchain is a series of interconnected blocks that store data. The form of Blockchain determines the Data that is contained inside a block.

Blockchain Is the Chain of Blocks That Contain Data

A Bitcoin Block, for example, includes details regarding the receiver, the sender, and the number of Bitcoins to be exchanged. The Genesis block is the first link in the chain. Every new block throughout the chain is connected to the one before it.

Understanding SHA256 - Hash

A hash is often a part of a block. A hash be thought of as a special fingerprint for each block. It uniquely distinguishes a block and all of its contents, similar to a fingerprint. As a result, if a block is generated, any alteration inside the blocks will change the Hash. As a result, the Hash is extremely useful for detecting shifts in intersections. If a block's fingerprint shifts, it is no longer the very same block. Every block has:

- Hash

- Data

- Hash of the previous block

Take into account the accompanying figure, and we have a sequence of 3 blocks. The first block seems to have no precursor. Thus, it does not include has the block header. Block 2 incorporates a hash of previous block 1. Although block 3 includes Hash of block 2. Hence, both blocks are carrying hashes of the preceding block.

This is the method that ensures the security of a Blockchain. Let's take a look at how it works. Assume an intruder has the ability to alter the data in block 2. As a result, the block's Hash shifts as well. However, block three also holds the block 2 Hash. As a result, block three and all subsequent blocks are null since the previous block's Hash is incorrect. As a result, modifying one block will easily render all subsequent blocks null.

Consensus Algorithms and Cryptocurrency

Consensus Algorithm

The consensus is a process that helps users and/machines communicate. It requires making sure that certain elements in the scheme will rely on a common point of fact, even though certain agents struggle. Thus, the mechanism must remain stable. In a hierarchical arrangement, there is a common authority that rules and decides, dictating how things are done.

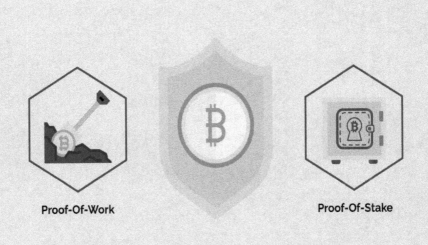

Proof-Of-Work   Proof-Of-Stake

In most instances, they will make modifications whenever they please. Any dynamic governance mechanism for finding agreement between multiple administrators is absent. But when distributed, it's another matter altogether. In a distributed ledger, how should we decide what entries should be entered? Overcoming this hurdle where people had difficulty trusting each other has been the most important step for Blockchains.

Cryptocurrencies and ledgers depend on consensus algorithms in this paper. In cryptocurrencies, the balances are held in a distributed ledger. It is important that any (or every) node retains an equivalent database. Otherwise, you could wind up with contradictory facts and undermine the network. No user is able to invest another's coins. In order for the network members to know what funds were invested, it must be in a single location.

The founder of Bitcoin, Satoshi, suggested a method of PoW. Its explanation will be given. Let's describe several of the various consensus algorithms. Validators must have a stake in the network to start. The validator seeks to prevent fraud by offering a stake in the ground. They would be severely punished if found cheating.

Examples cover computation and cryptocurrencies. Why should they put themselves at risk? Often, a reward is given. Fees for this typically provide a mix of the protocol's unique cryptocurrency and freshly-generated units of cryptocurrency.

Transparency

We don't need more openness to know that somebody is dishonest. For best security, blocks should be difficult to manufacture but easy to verify. It establishes that the identification process is controlled by users.

Important Real-Life Use Cases of Blockchain

Dubai: The Smart City

In 2016, the smart Dubai office implemented a Blockchain plan. Entrepreneurs and creators would be able to communicate with investors and leading firms through this technology. The aim is to incorporate a Blockchain-based infrastructure that encourages the growth of a variety of industries in order to render Dubai "the happiest city on the planet."

Incent Customer Retention

Incent is a Blockchain-based Consumer Retention as a Service platform. It's a rewards scheme that works by creating tokens for businesses that are part of the network. Blockchain is shared instantly in this scheme, and it can be placed in digital portfolios on a user's phone or accessed through a browser.

Blockchain for Humanitarian Aid

The UNWFP launched a humanitarian relief program in January 2017. The project was created in Pakistan's Sindh province's rural areas. Beneficiaries obtained capital, food, and all types of transactions are recorded on a Blockchain to maintain the process's protection and accountability.

Consensus Algorithms and Its Types

Proof-of-Work

The longest consensus algorithms are PoW. They were first used in Bitcoin. However, they have existed for quite some time now. The process by which validators (miners) attempt to hash the information before they arrive at a solution. A hash function is computed, and the hash value is generated as you pass the data through it. And if you repeat the experiment, you can still get the same result. It would be a minor detail to change even a single of your Hash.

Thus prove that you know that the data prior to the reality. After revealing the value, they will run the Hash on the data to ensure that it's the result is right. PoW lays down rules for what constitutes a legitimate block. Just the block starting with the number 'oo' will be approved. They will be able to change the criterion in any guess before getting to the right answer. The bar has been raised very high for big Blockchains. You'd need storage full of specific hashing hardware to deal with other miners and then some hope for generating a legitimate block.

When mining, the expense of these computers and the energy used to power them is your stake. Since ASICs are designed for a single-use, they can't be used for anything else. The only option to recoup the initial expenditure is to mine. Mining pays off handsomely if you connect a new transaction to the chain successfully. It's simple for the database to check that you've made the correct block.

You would need to pass the data through the feature once, even though you've attempted trillions of iterations to get the correct Hash. Your data would be approved if it generates a correct hash, and you will be rewarded. Otherwise, the system will deny it, and you will have squandered time and energy.

Proof-of-Stake

It was suggested as an option to PoW in the early days of Bitcoin. There are no miners, advanced hardware, or huge energy demand in a PoS device. What you'll require is a standard computer. Not all, to be sure. You do need to bring some money down. It is of little use to provide external assistance in a PoS. Instead, you put forward an internal cryptocurrency. Per protocol has its own set of rules, but in general, you must have a certain number of funds to be considered for staking. Then, when you have coins in a pouch, the funds are safe and not moveable (when you're staking, the coins are secure and immovable).

You and the other validators will usually compromise on which transactions will be used in the next block. You're betting on which block will be chosen, and the procedure will pick one for you. If you want a cut of the transaction costs depending on your contribution, you will be billed based on a percentage of your investment. You stand to make more money if you have more money tied away. You'll risk a majority (or all) of your stake if you want to cheat and offer invalid transactions. As a result, a system analogous to PoW is available, in which behaving fairly is more lucrative than being dishonest.

In certain cases, validators do not get newly produced coins as compensation. As a result, the Blockchain's indigenous currency must be created in another way, which can be accomplished by an initial delivery or by launching the protocol with Proof-of-Work before switching to PoS later. Simple PoS has only been seen in smaller cryptocurrencies thus far. As a result, it's unknown if it'll be a feasible option for PoW.

Although it seems to be sound, in theory, it can be different in reality. As PoS is implemented with an amount of significant value, the mechanism transforms into financial rewards. Anyone with some basic skills to hack any PoS machine would do it only if they stood to earn anything from it. So, the only place to see if it's possible is through a live database network. PoS will be put to the test on a wide scale shortly.

More Consensus Algorithms

All the algorithms have been focused on Proof-of-Work (POW) and Proof-of-Stake (PoS). There are plenty of reasons why anyone might use it, though, all of which have their own merits and demerits. Mechanisms for unity are central to distributed systems since, without them, a network would fall apart. Most Bitcoin enthusiasts think that the best thing about it is the PoW algorithm that allows users to settle on a single collection of truth.

Consensus algorithms nowadays support not only electronic cash networks but Blockchains, enabling developers to execute technology through a distributed system. They've been a pillar of Blockchain technologies and are essential for the lasting survival of existing networks. PoW continues to be the most common consensus algorithm among all of them. There is still to be suggested a more accurate and stable solution. However, there is a lot of development and research going into PoW substitutes, and we're sure to see even more in the future.

Blockchain 2.0 Has Given Users Some Great New Possibilities for Its Uses

When Nakamoto first published the Bitcoin whitepaper, it appeared that the technology would only be used with digital currency, but with the introduction of version 2.0, different usage cases have emerged on a daily basis.

Supply chain, investing, monitoring, and the Internet of Things are only a couple of the various implementations of Blockchain 2.0. Essentially, Blockchain 2.0 goes beyond exchanges by allowing people to share value without the use of a third-party broker.

Blockchain Has Been Compared by Many to the Internet

The Internet, like Blockchain technologies, was built piece by piece through the cooperation of several individuals and organizations, all of whom contributed valuable and meaningful contributions.

- Tim Berners-launch Lee's of www was the last landmark that helped propel the Internet into the organization we recognize today. This did not render him the Internet's master, and the same can be said about Nakamoto. Many software and programs are created and operated on the Internet nowadays, and their owners do not control the Internet; however, they own the program or service in question.

- The Blockchain resembles the early days of the Internet in several ways. Many people are considering what they should construct on the Blockchain, much as they were in the 1990s when any clever and technologically inclined individual was dreaming about creating such stuff on the Internet.

Anything from email to mates, commerce, and entertainment has made its way into the Internet, and we would expect Blockchain technologies to follow suit. Although no one controls Blockchain technology in and of itself, it may be argued that whoever has the most consumers owns the Blockchain practically. In the same manner, as certain internet behemoths can claim to be the Internet, Blockchain will be able to claim this title in the future.

Blockchains as Financial Market Infrastructures (FMIs)

We're really enthusiastic about the potential of emerging technology and how it could affect financial markets. Blockchain, or more broadly distributed ledger technology, is one of these innovations that has piqued our interest (DLT). Although we are extremely optimistic regarding DLT, we may not believe that it is a panacea for every sector, especially financial markets.

Recently, it has become clearer that Blockchains and cryptocurrency would not be able to completely overtake banks since these entities do far more than structured ledgers. Some attention has turned to how (and if) this software—or any technology, for that matter—may be used to dislodge the institutions that sit between banks and financial sector infrastructures (FMIs). We've invested a lot of time thinking about this, and we've written about it.

Before getting too busy, it's a good idea to review the initialisms and acronyms and understand what FMI is and what they do. In the 2012 Principles for Financial Markets Infrastructure, the Bank for Foreign Settlements (BIS) and the International Association of Securities Commissions (IOSCO) describe FMI (PFMI). The PFMI defines five distinct types of FMI companies and suggests regulatory standards for each:

Payment Systems (PS)

It is a compilation of "instruments, processes, and regulations for the movement of funds between or from participants; the scheme involves the participants as well as the body that operates the arrangement."

Central Securities Depositories (CSD)

It offers asset services, central safekeeping services, and securities accounts, which may involve the management of corporate activities and redemptions, and it plays a critical role in ensuring the credibility of securities concerns (that is, ensuring that securities are not produced, lost, or their data altered by mistake or fraudulently).

Securities Settlement Systems

It aids in the "transfer and settlement of shares by book entry in accordance with a series of predetermined significantly higher rules."

Central Counterparties

It serves as a middleman for counterparties of contracts sold on one or more capital exchanges, acting as a buyer for every seller and a seller for every buyer, ensuring that transparent contracts are fulfilled.

Trade Repositories

A consolidated electronic database of transaction records is maintained by this agency. What's crucial to remember is that the PFMI aren't laws or legislation in and of themselves; rather, they serve as a foundation for many regulators to create their own rules for the sector. There's also a difference to be made between an FMI's operational position (such as exchanging shares for settlement and their role as market operator overseer).

The above enables markets to deal with problems including settlement finality and default control, as well as crucial aspects like business regulation, a legal framework for applying settlements made inside (moving from the excessively simple "code is law"), and accountability. A cryptocurrency and Blockchain network like Bitcoin, at the most basic stage, has certain features that are similar to those offered by some of these FMIs. Bitcoin performs the rudimentary role of a CSD by keeping track of all value units on the Blockchain.

This role is supplemented by the opportunity to guarantee that Bitcoins are not fraudulently made or deleted from the network and that their data are not inappropriately modified, thanks to the mining mechanism (sent). Beyond its status as a CSD, Bitcoin may be argued to have a feature that functions similarly to an SSS. Note that I believe Bitcoin is more akin to an SSS than a PS since it guarantees anything that resembles the distribution of Bitcoin in a transaction after authentication by a miner, which is provided by an SSS but not always by a PS.

An SSS's operations essentially enable protection to be transferred from one party to another. Both users in Bitcoin may make a transaction to submit Bitcoins to other addresses in the scheme, and these transactions are validated and effectively exchanged until they are included in a mined block. Although these features, which, it should be remembered, perform well with a basic commodity like Bitcoin, it is difficult to believe that they can have any of the features needed to sustain transaction bandwidth or asset depth in a smaller financial sector.

However, and even more significantly, Blockchains lack many of the basic building blocks needed to create a large-scale industry. It's difficult to envision regulators allowing the elimination of the need for CSDs, SSSs, or PSs as legal entities if the technology of a massive CSD and SSS (as well as PS) were to switch to DLT(s)—something we think is feasible. Furthermore, consumers of these programs will check out the extra guarantees that certain organizations have, providing for redress both when things go bad and when something good happens. It is highly possible that those companies may not always be the incumbents, as has happened in other sectors. CSDs, SSSs, and PSs' business models would certainly need to adapt if DLT overcomes current technical barriers and gains broader acceptance by industry practitioners, in our opinion.

For example, a CSD will no longer be required to keep track of who holds what, but it will have to guarantee that the assets kept on a decentralized ledger are legitimate and that if an issuer defaults or takes corporate action against assets held on the Blockchain, the CSD will ensure the assets are removed or replaced in a timely manner. Beyond the CSD and SSS/PS features, Bitcoin does not actually, and perhaps never will provide the operating capabilities that CCPs provide (or even TRs).

More advanced public Blockchains, such as Ethereum, have rudimentary CCP functions that allow for trade maintenance through smart contracts and oracles. These organizations operate primarily to control and mutualize default liability in the case that a counterparty is unable to fulfill its commitments, including the right to sell on margin. Efforts to decentralize this would either sacrifice its essential functionality or would entail complete pre-funding, the costs and logistics of which will be daunting if not impractical for any large financial sector.

Over and beyond its basic features, a CCP's position in ensuring that only the most liquid, credit-worthy companies are permitted to engage in trades should not be overlooked. Several financial shocks have bolstered regulators' ability to shift more risk into these institutions. The emphasis now on how this might be best handled by these organizations, rather than encouraging a return to the previous paradigm.

Our inference is that these CCPs will profit from moving their infrastructure to a DLT, not just in terms of cost savings but also in terms of enabling them to perform their company in a more capital effective and much more open way, as well as providing them with the resources to manage the markets they regulate. Taken a step forward, a DLT could include a multi-purpose FMI forum for registered and controlled companies to transport and control properties and contracts with on behalf of their clients if they are merged on a shared platform run by several FMIs.

Furthermore, with the way a DLT can be designed, we think there is a chance that such a network might be built in such a way that it could be extremely standard remote. This means that even if a CSD or CCP operating their company on this site went bankrupt, the underlying DLT's reputation would be preserved, and an administrator might transfer the business to a stable organization.

The ability to build the next generation, multi-purpose business technology network utilizing DLT in a way that allows FMIs and their clients to work in a more reliable, less disruptive fashion is the whole justification for using Blockchains, in our opinion. It will be difficult, and it will not happen overnight; incumbents in these industries must have an open mind and constantly participate in the creation of a good experience for themselves, along with their customers.

Initial Coin Offering

The cryptocurrency industry's version of an initial public offering is an initial coin offering. An ICO is a method of raising funds for the creation of a new app, coin, or service.

Interested buyers will purchase the offering in exchange for a new token of cryptocurrency that the business has created. This token could be useful for using the company's services or products, or it could simply be a stake in exchange for the product or initiative.

- ICOs are a common funding tool for startups who want to sell goods and services in the Blockchain or cryptocurrency room.

- Initial coin offerings (ICOs) are equivalent to bonds, but they may often be used to fund a software device or service.

- Some initial coin offerings (ICOs) have resulted in huge profits for investors. Many more have failed, been exposed as frauds, or have done badly.

- In order to invest in initial coin offerings, you'll need to first buy a virtual currency and possess a good knowledge about how to utilize cryptocurrency exchanges and wallets.

- Since ICOs are mostly uncontrolled, investors must proceed with extreme vigilance and precaution when investigating and making investments in them.

Workings of Initial Coin Offering

When a company associated with cryptocurrency seeks to raise funds with an initial coin offering (ICO), it normally produces a whitepaper that explains what that particular project is all about, what is the need for the project would serve after it is completed, how much funding is required, how much digital tokens the creators can hold, what kind of capital would be allowed, and also for what period of time the campaign would last.

During the initiative of coin offering, project backers and fans purchase any of the project's tokens using digital currencies. The buyers refer to these coins as tokens, and they are equivalent to stock in a business offered to investors and members during an initial public offering. If the funds collected fall short of the firm's minimum requirements, the money could be transferred back to the benefactors; at this stage, the ICO is considered a failure. The money collected is utilized to fulfill the project's priorities, provided the financing criteria are fulfilled within the prescribed timeline.

Special Considerations

Those investors who are interested in investing in initial coin offerings (ICOs) can first become acquainted with the cryptocurrency field in general. Most ICOs require investors to buy tokens using cryptocurrencies that are pre-existent. This suggests that ICO investors would require a wallet for different currencies like Ethereum or Bitcoin and a wallet with the ability to store the currency or token they choose to buy. How should a person go about looking for ICOs to invest in?

Blockchain Fundamentals

It is not easy to keep up with the new ICOs. Reading up on potential ventures online is the smartest thing an active investor might do. ICOs cause a lot of buzz. There are a lot of sites online where investors meet to talk about potential prospects. There are websites devoted to obtaining ICOs., enabling investors to learn about new offers and equate them to each other.

ICO vs. IPO

Traditional businesses have a few options for collecting the funds they need for expansion and growth. A business will start smartly and then expand when its sales enable, with just the company owners as its creditors. This, though, implies that they are going to have to wait for resources to accumulate.

Companies will often seek early funding from outside buyers, which can provide them with a swift infusion of cash in exchange for a part of their equity interest. Another choice is to raise funds from private investors by trading stock in an initial public offering (IPO) and going public. While IPOs only deal with contributors, ICOs, including crowdfunding events, can deal with investors who would be interested in investing in new projects.

However, ICOs vary from Kickstarter in that ICO supporters are driven by the potential for a return or profit on their expenditure, while crowdfunding projects are essentially donations. That is why ICOs are called "crowd sales." It is interesting that ICOs still maintain at minimum two significant structural distinctions from IPOs. ICOs are essentially uncontrolled, implying that regulatory agencies like the Exchange and Securities Commission do not control them.

Second, ICOs are far more structure-free than IPOs owing to their decentralized structure and absence of oversight. ICOs may be arranged in a number of different forms. In certain situations, an organization will establish a particular fundraising target or cap, which ensures that every token traded through ICO will have a predetermined price, and the overall token supply will remain constant. In other scenarios, the ICO token supply is fixed, but the funding target is elastic.

This implies that the number of tokens distributed to holders would be determined by the funds collected. Others, on the other hand, provide a complex token supply that is calculated by the sum of funding collected. In both cases, the value of a token is set, but the total number of tokens is infinite.

Pros and Cons of ICO

In an initial public offering, the investor usually receives stock of a company's stock in return for her money. There are no securities per se in matters of an ICO. Instead, businesses collecting funds via an ICO issue a cryptocurrency token, which is the Blockchain approximation of a bond. In certain instances, investors swap a common current token, such as Ethereum or Bitcoin, for an equal quantity of new tokens.

It's worth remembering that it is quite simple for an organization to build tokens with an ICO. Online services make it possible to generate cryptocurrency tokens immediately. When comparing the variations between stocks and tokens, investors should bear this in mind. A token has no inherent worth and no ethical protections. ICO administrators create tokens in accordance with the conditions of the ICO, collect them and assign them to individual investors accordingly as per their schedule.

Early participants in ICOs are typically enticed to purchase tokens hoping that the venture can prosper until it is launched. If this occurs, the valuation of different tokens they bought during an ICO will rise above the value set during an ICO, resulting in net profits. The opportunity for extremely large returns is the major advantage of an ICO. Many holders have become millionaires as a result of ICOs. With the rise of ICOs in the Blockchain and cryptocurrency markets, they've taken with them new obstacles, threats, and opportunities. Many people invest in ICOs to get a fast and efficient profit on their money.

The most popular initial coin offerings (ICOs) of the last few years have proven to be the basis of this optimism since they have delivered enormous profits. This zeal, on the other hand, has the potential to drive citizens astray. ICOs are fraught with scams and con artists seeking to exploit overly zealous and ill-educated buyers as they are mostly uncontrolled. Funds missing due to theft or negligence can never be restored because they are not supervised by financial regulators such as the SEC. A couple of years back, a number of legislative and private bodies reacted to the meteoric growth of ICOs in 2017.

A couple of major Chinese Banks outlawed the use of tokens as currencies and forbade banks from providing ICO-related services. As a consequence, both Ethereum and Bitcoin rates plummeted, fueling speculation that further Blockchain legislation was on the way. The prohibition often applied to offerings that had already been initiated. ICO ads were blocked by Twitter, Facebook, and Google in early 2018. When it comes to ICOs, you can't be sure that as an investor, you would not become a victim of fraud. Investors should take the following precautions to prevent ICO scams:

- Ascertain that project planner may accurately identify their objectives. Whitepapers for successful ICOs are usually easy, understandable, and have specific, succinct objectives.

- Get to know the programmers. Investors should expect an organization introducing an ICO to be fully transparent.

- Look into the ICO's legitimate conditions and terms. Since outside authorities seldom monitor this industry, it is up for the preference of investors to guarantee that any ICO they participate in is legal.

Ascertain, the ICO assets are kept in one or more escrow account, which is a wallet that can only be opened with multiple keys. This will help protect you from scams, particularly if any of the keys are held by an impartial third party.

Advantages and Disadvantages of Blockchain

Through its difficulty, Blockchain's ability as a decentralized record-keeping system is almost limitless. Blockchain technology can have benefits beyond those mentioned above, ranging from increased consumer safety and protection to lower transaction costs and fewer mistakes. However, there are several drawbacks.

Advantages of Blockchain

- Reduced costs by reducing third-party authentication.
- Transactions are safe, confidential, and effective.
- Open technology.
- Decentralization allows it more difficult to tamper with.
- Provides a banking solution and a way to secure private info for residents in countries with insecure or underdeveloped regimes.

Accuracy of the Chain

A network of multiple machines approves transactions mostly within the Blockchain network. This virtually eliminates human intervention in the verification phase, resulting in lower human error and a more reliable record of data.

And if one of the computers on the network had a cryptographic error, it would only affect one copy of the ledger. To propagate to the majority of the Blockchain, the mistake will have to be rendered by at least 51% of

49

the network's machines, which is almost impossible in a massive and network like Bitcoin's.

Cost Reductions

Consumers typically pay a bank to validate a contract, a notary to sign a certificate or a priest to marry them. The Blockchain reduces the need for third-party authentication, as well as the costs that come with it.

When businesses receive credit card fees, for example, they must pay a nominal charge to banks and money service providers to handle the purchases. Bitcoin, on the other side, has no overarching jurisdiction and just has a small number of transaction fees.

Decentralization

Blockchain doesn't keep all the data in a single region. Instead, a network of machines copies and spreads the Blockchain. Any device on the network updates its database to represent the addition of a new block to the Blockchain.

Blockchain makes it more impossible to tamper with data by disseminating it through a network rather than maintaining it in a single central database. If a programmer obtained a snapshot of the Blockchain, only a single copy of the data will be corrupted, rather than the whole network.

Efficient Transactions

The settlement of transactions made by a central authority will take many days. For example, if you deposit a check on Friday night, you cannot see money in the account until Monday. Blockchain operates 24 hours a day, seven days a week, and throughout the year, while financial companies run within business hours, five days a week.

Transactions may be done in as little as ten minutes, and after just a few hours, they are deemed stable. This is especially useful for cross-border transactions, which take even longer due to time zone differences and the requirement that both parties validate payment delivery.

Private Transactions

Most Blockchain networks function as public libraries, allowing anybody with an internet link to access the network's recent transactions. While users have access to transaction data, they do not have access to identifiable information regarding the users that are conducting the transactions.

It's a widespread misconception that public Blockchains like Bitcoin are private when they're not. That is, rather than their personal details, a user's unique code, known as a public key, is stored on the Blockchain when they make public transactions.

A person's identity is always attached to their Blockchain address whenever they made a Bitcoin purchase on an exchange that needs authentication. However, a sale, except though bound to a person's name, would not disclose any personal details.

Secure Transactions

The Blockchain network must verify the validity of a transaction after it has been registered, and thousands of machines on the Blockchain scramble to verify that the purchase's facts are right. The transaction is applied to the Blockchain block after it has been checked by a machine. Every block has its own unique hash, as well as the hash of the previous block. The hashCode of a block varies as the information on it is changed in some way; however, the hashCode of the block after it does not. Because of this disparity, changing details on the Blockchain without warning is exceedingly challenging.

Transparency

The majority of Blockchains are made up completely of open-source applications. This ensures that anybody with access to the internet will look at the code. This allows auditors to check the reliability of cryptocurrencies, including Bitcoin. This also implies that no real jurisdiction exists on who owns Bitcoin's code or how it is edited.

As a result, everyone may propose device improvements or modifications. Bitcoin will be upgraded if a number of network users believe that the latest version of the code with the change is sound and worthwhile.

Banking the Unbanked

The opportunity for anybody, regardless of race, gender, or cultural context, to use Blockchain and Bitcoin is perhaps its most significant feature. According to the World Bank, almost 2 billion adults lack bank accounts or any other way of holding their money or assets. Almost all of these people reside in developed nations, where the country is already in its infancy and money is king.

These individuals also receive small amounts of money and are compensated in cash. They must then hide this

Blockchain Fundamentals

tangible cash in their homes or places of business, making them vulnerable to extortion or needless

abuse. A Bitcoin wallet's keys can be written down, saved on a cheap mobile phone, or even memorized if appropriate.

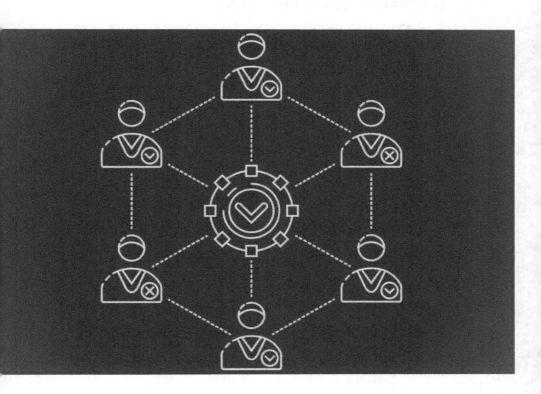

These solutions are more likely to be hidden than a little bundle of money under a mattress for most people. Blockchains in the future are now searching for ways to hold medical documents, land ownership, and a host of other civil transactions, in addition to being a unit of account for asset storage.

Disadvantages of Blockchain

While the Blockchain has a lot of benefits, it still has a lot of drawbacks when it comes to acceptance. Today's roadblocks to Blockchain technology adoption aren't only technological. For the most part, the real obstacles are political and legislative, not to mention the thousands of hours of custom product development and back-end programming needed to incorporate Blockchain into existing enterprise networks. The following are some of the roadblocks to universal Blockchain acceptance.

- Bitcoin mining has a high infrastructure cost.
- Bitcoin has a history of being used in illegal activities.
- Transactions per second are low.
- Legislation.

Technology Cost

Although Blockchain will save users resources on transaction costs, it is not a free technology. Bitcoin's "Proof-of-Work" scheme, for example, consumes a tremendous amount of computing resources to verify transactions.

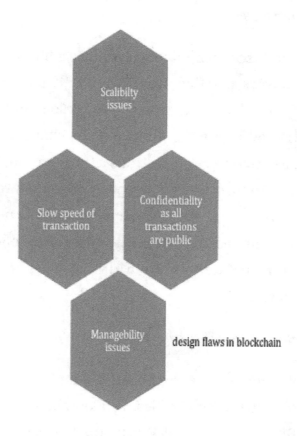

design flaws in blockchain

In the real world, the power generated by the Bitcoin network's millions of computers is roughly equivalent to Denmark's annual electricity use. Assuming energy costs of $0.03~$0.05 per kWh, operating costs exclusive of hardware expenditures are around $4,000 to $6,000 per coin. Despite the high costs of mining cryptocurrency, consumers want to pump up their utility bills in order to verify transactions on the network.

That's so when miners introduce a block to the Bitcoin network, and they are credited with just enough Bitcoin to render their time and resources worthwhile. However, miners will need to be charged or otherwise incentivized to verify transactions on Blockchains that do not use cryptocurrencies. Any answers to these problems are starting to emerge. Bitcoin mining farms, for example, have been set up to utilize solar electricity, waste natural gas from drilling sites, or wind farm power.

Speed Inefficiency

Bitcoin is an excellent example of Blockchain's potential inefficiencies. It takes about ten minutes for Bitcoin's "Proof-of-Work" method to connect a new block to the Blockchain. The Blockchain can only handle about seven payments a second at that point, according to estimates (TPS).

Other cryptocurrencies, such as Ethereum, outperform Bitcoin, but they are also constrained by Blockchain. For example, the legacy Visa brand will manage 24,000 transactions per second. For years, people have been working on solutions to this issue. There are Blockchains that can handle over 30,000 transactions per second right now.

Illegal Activity

While the Blockchain network's anonymity prevents people from hacking and maintains their secrecy, it also allows for illicit trade and operation. The Silk Road, an encrypted "Dark Web" drug marketplace that operated from February 2011 until October 2013, when it was shut down by the FBI, is perhaps the most well-known case of Blockchain being used for illegal transactions.

Using the TOR browser, users may search the website without being watched and making illicit Bitcoin and other cryptocurrency transactions. Financial service companies must collect details about their customers before they open an account, check each customer's identification, and ensure that customers may not exist on any registry of confirmed or alleged terrorist groups, according to current US regulations.

This method has both advantages and disadvantages. It encourages everyone to enter financial accounts, but it still makes it easier for offenders to trade. Many have claimed that the positive uses of cryptocurrency, such as financing the unbanked, outweigh the negative uses, particularly because the majority of criminal activity is still carried out with untraceable cash.

Regulation

Many people in the crypto community are worried about government oversight of cryptocurrencies. Governments could potentially render it unlawful to hold cryptocurrency or invest in their networks, despite the fact that ending anything like Bitcoin is becoming extremely complicated and near impossible when the decentralized network develops. As major corporations, including PayPal, continue to promote the possession and usage of cryptocurrency on their platforms, this issue has diminished.

Blockchain's Advances Rely on Scalability

Scalability, or the opportunity to accomplish transactions in almost real-time, like clearing credit card purchases, is one of the key challenges confronting Blockchain. With cryptocurrencies like Bitcoin and Ethereum's Ether, scalability has already been described as an issue. If a distributed ledger is to gain traction among financial technology (FinTech) firms and contend with payment networks dozens of times faster, it must improve scalability and throughput while also addressing latency issues.

Enter "Sharding"

Developers are experimenting with a number of approaches to improve transactional throughput, including sharding. Simply placed, sharding is a method of partitioning a P2P network's computational and storage burden such that no one node is liable for the entire program's transaction-oriented workload. Instead, each node just keeps data about its own partition or shard.

The details in a shard will also be exchanged by other nodes, keeping the ledger decentralized and technically stable so anyone can access all ledger entries; they just don't process and archive all the information, such as bank transactions and contract code. Each authenticating machine or node in today's Blockchains documents all the data mostly on the electronic ledger and participates in the consensus phase.

In wide Blockchain technology such as Bitcoin, the majority of network parties must verify new transactions and document the data if they are to be added to the Blockchain; that makes processing each payment slow and laborious. Because of this and, Bitcoin, which is built on a PoW, can only handle 3.3 to 7 tps; and a financial document can take 10 to 15 minutes to complete. Ethereum, another widely used Blockchain database, and cryptocurrency can only handle 12 to 30 payments every second. VisaNet, on the other hand, handles 1,700 operations per second on average.

Chapter 2: Cryptocurrency and Crypto Assets

Bitcoin vs. Blockchain

The aim of the Blockchain is to make records visible and unalterable. The concept of Blockchain was first formulated in 1991 by two scholars who wished to make sure that documents could not be altered. But it wasn't till January 2009, almost two decades after the creation of Bitcoin, that Blockchain had its first deployment in the real world. The Bitcoin protocol is based on a distributed public ledger, also known as a Blockchain, a peer-to-peer system with no trusted third parties.

More important, in practice than in principle, Bitcoin simply utilizes a database as a way of transparently recording transfers. However, in the long term, it may potentially be used to store everything. In the discussions above, this can be related to sales, as well as commodity inventories, deeds to property, referendum votes, and so on. Currently, the overwhelming majority of Blockchain-based projects use it to support the community as a wide range of applications rather than just tracking transactions. A prime example of Blockchain use is that it is that of voting in democratic elections. Blockchain's immutable existence implies that election bribery would be more challenging.

An example of this is a voting scheme that will allow citizens of a nation to use a single token or cryptocurrency. Each nominee will be granted a special wallet address, and the electors would make a contribution in whatever currency they want. Any ballot would be clear and unalterable, and the chain of custody (the logical record of votes cast) would prevent the possibility of vote tampering.

Blockchain vs. Banks

Banks and Blockchains vary greatly to discover how a bank varies from Bitcoin's application of Blockchain, compare the method to the banking sector.

Bitcoin and other cryptocurrencies are digital tokens that are not protected by actual money or physical securities. They are exchanged between willing parties without the use of a middleman and are recorded on digital ledgers. Cryptocurrency can be regarded best as digital currency or simulated currency protected by encryption, making counterfeiting and double-spending virtually impossible. Many cryptocurrencies are focused on Blockchain technology, a public database implemented by a distributed network of computers.

Cryptocurrencies are distinguished because they are not distributed by any central entity, making them technically resistant to political intervention or coercion. A cryptocurrency is a modern kind of digital commodity built on a network that spans a vast number of computers. They can operate independently of the jurisdiction of the government and central authorities because of their autonomous nature. The term "cryptocurrency" comes from the encryption mechanisms used to keep the network stable.

Many cryptocurrencies rely on Blockchains, which are organizational methods for preserving the accuracy of transactional data. Blockchain and associated technologies, according to several analysts, would change many markets, including finance and law. Cryptocurrencies have been chastised for various factors, including their usage for illicit activity, exchange rate fluctuations, and the technology that underpins them becoming vulnerable.

Their inflation, divisibility, resistance, portability, and transparency, on the other hand, have been lauded. Cryptocurrencies are online payment schemes that are collateralized in terms of abstract "tokens" defined by ledger entries on the system's internal ledger. Various encryption methods and cryptographic mechanisms, such as elliptic curves encryption, hashing functions, and private-public key pairs, are referred to as "crypto."

Fundamentals of Cryptocurrency

Most investors have no idea if Bitcoin is money, an asset, a safe, or anything completely different. Economists point out that Bitcoin's worth is subject to "indeterminacy." It is based on self-fulfilling expectations, and the number of beliefs that can be self-fulfilling is enormous. To put it another way, the underlying generators of Bitcoin's valuation might as well be sunspots.

Bitcoin has developed a reputation as digital gold. This explains why Bitcoin is so appealing to buyers, as well as how its historical gains and lack of correlation render it a good addition to every portfolio. Investors are also far from being willing to understand that $10,000 is a decent deal or explains the wild price fluctuations. This void can make it difficult to invest in cryptocurrency exchanges, but it also provides an incentive for analysts who are willing to experiment with new valuation approaches and fundamentals.

This whitepaper is prepared for those researchers and their colleagues, and it provides an overview of principles and measures that can help with crypto asset valuation. We don't claim to have any formulas; instead, we believe that by drawing on ideas like the ones we've presented here, visionary investors and analysts can achieve an advantage. Our review is not intended to be exhaustive since the world of crypto research is rapidly changing, with new metrics and approaches appearing every week; this is only one of the many reasons that render this sector so appealing to analysts and skilled investors.

Bitcoin and Ether as Commodities

Now we'll look at the valuation proposition for Bitcoin and ether, the Ethereum network's native crypto asset. We'll try to explain how narratives centered on commodity trading analogies are gaining traction. These analogies show how to calculate the supply and demand for Bitcoin and Ethereum's money, ether. Identifying supply curves and the dynamics that underpin demand is critical for arriving at a quantifiable valuation.

Bitcoin as Digital Gold

Interest in Bitcoin's use in global trade and in the digitized financial sector was highlighted in 2019, but now that Bitcoin is defined as a "digital asset that is impossible to grab, freeze, confiscate, or reduce in value," that is what it is. Investors recognize the global need for such an asset, and governments are as well as big as small and so prone to use government debt as a tool to save industries in periods of economic distress.

In contrast to traditional money, Bitcoin has a very little cost of custody and zero conversion costs, which makes it very suitable for transactions in the digital era. An understanding of the basic supply and demand laws that can be applied to gold prices is well in place. Despite having been in existence for a fraction of the time that gold has, Bitcoin lacks a lasting currency.

There are many issues with Bitcoin being a replacement for gold, the chief of which being its past, as it has only been around for a fleeting period of time. One way to look at what "Bitcoin-as-worth" will be, is to consider the perceived value of it if it were to go up to represent any proportion of the total demand for gold.

Ether as Digital Oil

Bitcoin splits the role of governing the money supply and distributes it to machines all around the world; Ethereum does the same with coding. The details and reasoning underlying an application were "decentralized" rather than being hosted on private servers. DApps, or "decentralized software," operate on the Ethereum protocol, which connects a global network of computers. Ether is a payment token that can be used to purchase computing space on the network.

Many who predict a rise in ether demand believe that decentralized apps would outperform centralized incumbents. This might happen if, for example, anti-Facebook rhetoric encourages people to check out alternate social networks that have more user-level data access and better privacy protections. In other terms, ether may be the information economy's gasoline.

A common fundamental criterion may be applicable to Ethereum and its many rival DApp networks, similar to how subscribers or active users calculate FAANG holdings. Since these networks' transactions are open to the media, this activity may be analyzed in real-time. So far, there's no proof that every Ethereum-based DApp is creating consumer demand on par with Facebook or the other FAANG firms.

Metrics to Track Demand for Digital Gold

Bitcoin and Ethereum, including services, do not produce revenue and must be assessed in terms of supply and demand. New metrics to be used on each side of the equation are also being developed and refined by analysts.

Price and market capitalization are insufficient. They can be deceiving in certain ways. Here are a few of those new metrics, along with an explanation of how they apply to Bitcoin. The majority of them even apply to ether and other crypto properties.

Metcalfe's Law

It states that the influence of a network is equal to the difference in the number of members and is named after Bob Metcalfe, the inventor of the Ethernet cable. In other terms, the importance of a network to its members grows logarithmically, not linearly, as new users join. The fax machine is a textbook example: two fax machines allow one possible contact path; four fax machines enable six.

Facebook has proof of this, with sales increases equal to the square of the number of users. Unfortunately, crypto-assets do not follow the same logic. The number of active domains is unrelated to the price of Bitcoin.

It shouldn't matter as Metcalfe's Law deals with effect, not merit. A greater network of fax machines increases the efficacy of each computer on the network; it does not mean a better benefit for each individual machine or for telecom services. A more nuanced interpretation of how Bitcoins are exchanged and stored is needed to assess the worth of a Bitcoin.

Transaction Volumes

The number of Bitcoin transactions is one indicator of its popularity. In this regard, Bitcoin is often pitted against more flexible payment networks such as Alipay, SWIFT, and the VISA service. But, like gold, we're talking of Bitcoin as just a store of cash. Coffee is not purchased with gold.

While Bitcoin performs fewer transactions than other commercial payment systems, the average transaction value is much higher. On a logarithmic scale, the chart below depicts Bitcoin's regular transaction volume development.

Bitcoin Days Destroyed

Though transaction amount may be fascinating, it doesn't really show how active the economy is. The moveability feature makes it easy for users to store vast amounts of Bitcoins in different Bitcoin accounts for their protection and convenience. First proposed in 2011, "Bitcoin balance days destroyed" indicates how much confidence users have in the Bitcoin holdings they have owned for a long time.

In the case of a user who moves 100 BTC after holding them for a period of 1,000 days, that is one Bitcoin destroyed or permanently removed from the economy. The sum of the amounts is still equal, except though the money is split up and distributed to different locations. It is useful because it eliminates some of the noise from transactions that result from management activities within the organization, providing a more accurate assessment of the actual economic activity.

Realized Cap

Other factors that affect the valuation of Bitcoin are the number of transactions and the amount of wealth deposited in it. Expanding is completed by the term "market capitalization" and does the math calculation and multiplying the stock by the number of securities remaining. While the math used to figure out the percentage gain of crypto assets that remain, be hidden, or not used is quite similar, that used by Bitcoin (2.6%) is just accounting for large losses and flaws at the time of 3.7 million BTC, according to a crypto analytics company.

The source uses the same statistics to estimate "realized" Bitcoin days destroyed to estimate "lost cap"; by crypto research company researcher advocates, a measure they term "realized Bitcoin days destroyed." The realized capitalization is a way of measuring the market capitalization depending on the valuation a Bitcoin holds at the moment of the most recent exchange.

When calculating a cost basis, the cost of each record on the date of purchase is considered. In this case, if a consumer made a purchase on July 1, 2011, her shares will be gauged to the market price on that date of $100,000 USD and are now $41, although some could have since been exchanged for more valuable Bitcoins.

Types of Cryptocurrency

At the time of writing, Bitcoin remains the most common and most valuable cryptocurrency ever built on Blockchain technology. Currently, there are thousands of cryptocurrencies that serve different purposes and requirements of varying features. A few of these cryptocurrencies are derivatives or forked versions of Bitcoin, although some are brand new currencies that were created from scratch.

"Satoshi Nakamoto" started the project in 2009 as an unknown entity and now uses the name "Satoshi Nakomoto" to identify himself/themselves. The estimated volume of all currently circulating in the industry is over $146 billion, with 18 million coins (18,000,000,000,000 BTC) being valued at $1 BTC. Any of the offspring from the projects which are attributable to Bitcoin's popularity is called "altcoins" such as Litecoin, Peercoin, and Namecoin, along with Ethereum and Cardano, and EOS. The estimated valuation of all cryptocurrencies combined now amounts to over $214 billion, which equates to approximately $68 billion of the total value of all cryptocurrencies.

Cryptography designed for military purposes has been re-forged to have a variety of uses in cryptocurrency. The current government had tried to place restrictive limits on cryptography close to those put in place on firearms, but it was realized that individuals should have the ability to own personal security based on the argument of the rights of citizens' freedoms.

Attributes of Cryptocurrency

Decentralization

To understand how Blockchain, it is valuable to look at the ways in which it is implemented by Bitcoin is helpful to look at another cryptocurrency as well. To put it another way, like a database, it needs a cluster of computers to store the Blockchain; Bitcoin has a Blockchain. This database is just tracking the details of any single Bitcoin transaction ever created for Bitcoin's Blockchain is just one example of a Bitcoin-specific database for now.

Each server, in this case, functions as part of a network rather than as opposed to being assigned to a single user. Unlike most databases, where all the machines are administered by one person or many users, this one does not. A network that's worth $10,000 has already included the personal records of a large organization has already been merged with the 10,000 machines in the company's servers.

The warehouse has these machines under one roof and has complete custody over each and every piece of knowledge of them. Similarly, in the case of Bitcoin, there are thousands of independent machines that run the network, each of which is spread out across the world in many various geographic locations, human or communal locations. A device that takes part in Bitcoin's network is known as "nodes." Instead of being used in a centralized fashion, the Blockchain is used in a decentralized manner in this model. A more limited yet commonly used alternative is a private Blockchain where the machines on the network are under the exclusive control and management of one person.

Any block on the block is full of information of its own creation is added, which gives the network the users and miners full access to the whole record of the transaction history since the inception of the Blockchain. Bitcoin has a data archive with any of all Bitcoin transactions recorded and stored within the

Blockchain. In the event of a single node containing inaccurate data, faulty or missing data, all the others will serve as references to use to determine or find the data.

Knowledge is not stored in either node on the network, meaning that no one entity in the network will corrupt it. The Blockchain consists of the past transaction background of Bitcoin. Because the Blockchain is irreversible, any block in the history of transactions cannot be changed; it is effectively the historical record of all that has occurred and the end of the Bitcoin project. If one person tampers with the log of transactions, all other nodes can be quickly pinpointed as well.

In this method, we are able to obtain an exact and completely detailed timeline of activities, enabling us to more easily understand what happened from start to finish. Transactions in a database: Bitcoin can store all financial and other kinds of records as well as legal and commodity details records, but other information such as government identifications and companies' product inventories can also be accommodated in the Blockchain.

In order to alter how the mechanism operates, or the knowledge contained inside it, a majority of the autonomous network's processing resources will need to vote on said improvements. This means that any improvements that do come remain in the best interests of the public.

Transparency

Decentralized by design, all Bitcoin transactions are made visible to all time and recorded in the public Blockchain and even can be viewable using a personal node, as well as network explorers. Per node maintains its own copy of the chain, which gets synchronized with the second the moment fresh blocks are checked and included in the chain. Along as you've got access to a Blockchain, you can follow Bitcoin everywhere you're willing to.

For instance, it's well known that Bitcoin exchanges have been targeted by hackers who gained access to the exchange and then completely robbed of their funds. It's easy for the hacker to remain anonymous. However, they would be able to get Bitcoins that can be traced. There would be no problem if the stolen Bitcoins were transferred or invested because the information that was used to steal them would be available.

What Is Cryptocurrency?

A cryptocurrency, like conventional currencies such as our dollar, is a mode of trade that is programmed to exchange digital knowledge via a mechanism enabled by cryptographic principles. A digital currency is categorized as a branch of alternate currency and virtual currencies.

Cryptocurrency is a cryptographic cryptography-based bearer instrument. In this type of cryptocurrency, the coin is owned by the person who holds it. There is no such record of the owner's name. Wei Dai released "B-Money," an anonymous, decentralized electronic cash method, in 1998.

Cryptocurrency and Blockchain

Cryptocurrencies, also known as virtual currency, are digital ways of trade that are secured through cryptography. The term "crypto" is derived from the Greek word "kryptós," which means "secret" or "private." There are several advantages to a digital currency that is developed and utilized by private entities or organizations.

Cryptocurrencies defy conventional wisdom on how money functions, which excites some but worries others. So, what is Bitcoin, and how would it vary from other forms of payment?

Cryptocurrencies, unlike most coins, are completely digital. There are no cryptocurrencies that print money or mint coins. Anything is achieved via the internet. Governments create traditional types of money, which are then exchanged throughout the economy through banks.

Value of a Cryptocurrency

Cryptocurrencies are independent of any of these organizations. Cryptocurrency, on the other hand, is decentralized. In other terms, its consumers are the ones that make, share, and control it. Cryptocurrencies are mined online. Mining precious minerals have long been used to have a monetary value.

The topic of how cryptocurrencies have value is complicated, but it shows that the value of every currency is derived from confidence in its purchasing ability. Any currency must have a scheme in place to prevent theft and misuse.

Blockchain

This is achieved in banking through ledgers that monitor money transfers across accounts. The mission is carried out using Bitcoin using Blockchain and a form of math known as cryptology. A Blockchain is a protected database of any single cryptocurrency transaction. As part of the mining method, verified transactions are applied to the Blockchain.

As a result, mining isn't all about making new money; it's also about validating transactions. Although cryptocurrency can be purchased, what you need is a digital wallet, which can be found as part of a free app or cryptocurrency tax program. Buying and selling of it are challenging due to the difficulty in finding locations that would allow it, as well as the variable processing fees and unpredictable exchange rates.

Valuing Crypto Assets beyond Bitcoin and Ether

Bitcoin might resemble virtual gold, and ether might resemble digital gasoline, but how about the thousands of other cryptocurrency exchanges? Some purport to deliver enhancements on the Bitcoin which Ethereum models and can be measured utilizing many of the same metrics mentioned above.

Others most strongly mimic patented currency, including game coins, arcade tokens, or cheques. There are various kinds of decentralized apps, including one that uses native assets for file storage and dental care. Stocks and bonds are an excellent measure of the long-term health of a company since they capture fortune changes in profits.

If a game token has the revenue of Chuck E. Cheese's, what will it be used for? It is now the view of some early crypto investors that decentralized applications (or DApps) could serve as an entry point of entry for cryptocurrency into the market. This list includes several of their previous works.

Crypto Assets as Tokens

We are concerned with capturing and enhancing the demand generated inside the market by charging for a commodity over the cost to produce. Applications that are decentralized may potentially have comparable value flows but have no point of monetary value. If you have the incentive of a third party, you will be taking away a third-party chance, and if you leave it out, you will be giving rise to the potential for rent-seeking middlemen to participate.

A recent development instead of analyzing these "Utility Tokens" has attempted to regard the network of asset investors as a multi-asset market, in which the number of ways in which assets are exchanged, μ, equals the quotient of the network, and nominal cash flows, (as opposed to average) v is called proprietary. In regard to this calculation, m is the supply of currency, the "velocity" (how many times money switches hands it appears) is a metric of how quickly it increases, "market level" or decreases (evaluated in the U.S. using the CPI), p is "the quantity of products and services," and q is the average "real money" value.

Prior to the ICOs of 2017, several token issuers failed to take note of this equation and have said that "utility tokens" are nothing more than worthless pieces of digital coupons or tokens. The concept of a patented currency was ignored due to the undervaluation of the usefulness of what they had found.

Expanding transaction: Expanded transactions indicate how fast individuals divest their funds and liquidate their holdings. Equal exchange holdings reflect on the calculation. Currency's maximum value is reached, but long-term prices fall because of increased supply; in other terms, high velocity is linked to falling prices. Losing a lot of gas means that this stock is likely to be very stable in the long term. Nobody can hold on to a Chuck E. Cheese token for an additional time period of time in 15 years.

Crypto Assets as Taxi Medallions

As a subtler way of thinking of how to interpret value, some investors have defined utility tokens as analogous to work-equity in that they grant their holders permission to use and benefit from the network they allow their creation of revenue Platform token holders must "lock tokens" to perform the functions that are part of their duties, which means they must retain assets to use them as collateral.

This means the availability or demand for assets in a 2-sided market will change at any moment, which impacts performance. Fund managers refer to this as a token work token and comment that use on the use of the network as the network's utility source that is central to it.

Blockchain Fundamentals

Crypto Assets as Governance

Relying on the idea that crypto-assets are a right to perform new tasks, certain investors suggest a new type of investing of which everybody will have a share. Underlying the traditional finance theories such as the freedom to participate, such as that the shareholder rights model, equity does not provide due consideration for liquidity rights, such as voting rights, and pricing stock exclusively dependent on future cash flows is disregarded.

Generally speaking, investors may have used their ability to own digital assets to secure return on investment (ROPS) to secure the retu Remove investment (ROI) goals, but the managers at their respective company proposed generalized mining (where a single coin grants infinite access to several types of investments). Instead of investing in shares of private companies, investors in Blockchain tokens may apply data science to decide the vehicles that produce the most revenue in the most value in decentralized Uber.

The service sector investor receives a return on the profit-making process that she is responsible for on the network. Placeholder often sees that the rise in the number of vehicles and ride-sharing trips raises the network's total "asset," the approach of which will have major implications for fundamental research. Because the transaction validation of each "miner" has to earn BTC requires extensive effort, the word "generalized mining" has been applied to Bitcoin to refer to miners that are referring to generalized.

Asset-backed designs need "validators" (who own stakes in the system), or they would only be able to receive some compensation. To receive a return, these types of employment are generally including participation and constructive participation. Skeptics also pointed out that there isn't much of a difference if one shorts stocks as well as long stocks. When people are involved with a product, their expectations go beyond just becoming customers.

This paradigm might have incentives to induce people to enter the market in non-expressive ways that don't aim to enhance the worth of the asset. No discussion of "regular buyers" and "doing work" investing in taxicabs/vehicle tracking should be considered alongside the speculation about whether/whether someone else, other than investors with sufficient investment capital would, will roll up their sleeves to get involved.

Applications and Benefits of Cryptocurrency

The way we do financial transactions could be totally altered through the use of cryptocurrency. Blockchain may be used in many industries that include confidence among various parties but can also be put into a further mechanism that has components, such as supply chain management, third-party payment processing, dispute resolution, legal, digital trust, and records management, and identity verification.

Blockchains hold data that is both safe and visible on the whole communities participating computers, allowing anyone to see and no one to tamper with or influence the knowledge in the chain. Exciting, to be sure, but how will it be done? Blocks may be another reason as well: for the simple fact that. Now, instead of a long array of dealing with an extensive series of data, the information in Blockchain information is broken up into enclosed chunks of blocks.

It is difficult to alter or counterfeit the documents in the block due to the use of cryptography. What's within these bricks, though? When offering an exclusive artwork, for example, you want the block to include details about the painting's name, the creator, the former owner, the current owner, the duration of the transfer, and the transaction. Each block has a recognizable hash next to the info. This is a one-of-a-kind code that works similarly to a fingerprint. One of the many advantages of cryptocurrencies being that it is decentralized and does not controlled by any governing body or bank, as making it resistant to political intervention or exploitation.

Blockchain Fundamentals

Getting a decentralized structure of command and control is referred to as having command and control with decentralization. With regards to a centralized economy, currencies, the government or corporation has full or partial control over currency control. It has two methods of currency distribution: currency (central banks and the government) and commodity.

It controls the overall money supply by using the two strategies: currency, plus exchange fees (government and the rate of printing). Decentralized currency exists in a currency system in which the value and availability of currency are governed by the decisions of users and are regulated by dynamic protocols implemented through the usage of a peer-to-peer network.

Bitcoin

In 2009, a pseudonymous person or organization proposed an automated payment mechanism that is built on peer-to-peer networks and backed by cryptographic evidence instead of reliance on third parties.

To avoid the appearance of issues such as double expenditure, Bitcoin transactions are registered and verified on a distributed ledger utilizing Blockchain technology, and which prevents someone from altering the transaction record. This transaction can be seen as being case responsive and is treated as an individual address, meaning everyone can use it to collect the coins associated with it.

Altcoins

There are also such cryptocurrencies other than Bitcoin, now known as "altcoins." Most altcoins hope to do one either of these things with Bitcoin: substitute it, or be much better than it.

Alternative cryptocurrencies can differ greatly from one another. However, at least one aspect is universal: quicker transaction speeds, private transaction histories, proof-of-stake methods, and multi-of-age verification.

Takeaway

All in all, cryptocurrencies have a long way to go until they will actually surpass today's currency and be embraced in world trade. When the majority of the world is able to consider cryptocurrencies as ordinary payment methods, only time will say.

What Is Mining?

Mining is the computer-assisted method of storing and checking data on the Blockchain, a distributed ledger. Since mining necessitates the usage of computing resources, people are paid to do it.

Each device that completes this procedure is qualified for a reward in digital currency and, on rare occasions, completely fresh, virgin coins. Just one block may be generated at a time to maintain the Blockchain network going smoothly. There are some options for doing so:

- The most general is evidence of operation, which requires machines to work diligently to solve a math problem. The first machine to solve this issue will create a new block and be able to add data to the Blockchain. They were rewarded with all new digital money as well as processing fees.

- Proof-of-Stake was the next mining strategy. The program selects individuals who display significant ownership of coins to build new blocks in this method. Competitors are chosen by a drawing scheme dependent on chance. There are no new coins produced with evidence of stake. Instead, payments are collected for checking and tracking transactions.

New methods of mining are being investigated and found as more than 700 cryptocurrencies are generated per month.

Special Considerations

Blockchain technology, which is used to hold an online database with any activities that have ever been conducted, thereby creating a data structure for this ledger that is very stable which is communicated and decided upon by the whole network of specific nodes, or computers holding a copy of the ledger, is central to the appeal and usefulness of Bitcoin and other cryptocurrencies.

A new block must be checked by each node before being authenticated, rendering forging transaction histories almost impossible. Many analysts believe that Blockchain technology has significant potential for applications such as online polling and fundraising, and large financial companies, including JPMorgan

Chase (JPM), believe that it has the potential to reduce transaction costs and streamline payment delivery.

However, since cryptocurrencies are digital and are not held in a central archive, the failure or collapse of a hard drive will wipe out a digital cryptocurrency balance if a backup copy of a private key is not kept. Around the same period, your assets and personal records are not accessible to any central jurisdiction, legislature, or company.

Advantages and Disadvantages of Cryptocurrency

Advantages

Cryptocurrencies have the potential to make it easy to change money between two parties without the use of a trustworthy third party such as a bank or card provider. Instead, these transactions are protected by the usage of public and private keys, as well as various reward schemes such as Proof-of-Work and Proof-of-Stake.

A customer's "wallet," or account address, in current cryptocurrency schemes, has a public key, whereas the private key is only identified by the user and is used to transact directly. Users will escape the high rates paid by customers and monetary firms for wire transactions by completing fund transfers with nominal transaction fees.

Disadvantages

Cryptocurrency transfers' semi-anonymous existence renders them ideal for a variety of illicit practices, including money laundering and tax evasion. Cryptocurrency supporters, on the other hand, also place a strong emphasis on confidentiality, claiming advantages such as security for whistleblowers and dissidents residing in oppressive regimes.

Such coins have a higher level of anonymity than others. Since cryptographic examination of the Bitcoin network has assisted police in arresting and prosecuting suspects, Bitcoin is a comparatively weak option for performing illicit business electronically. There are, however, more privacy-oriented coins like Dash, Monero, and ZCash that are much more difficult to track.

Criticism of Cryptocurrency

Since cryptocurrency market rates are determined by market forces, the rate at which a currency can be traded for another cryptocurrency can vary greatly, especially because several cryptocurrencies are designed to be scarce.

Bitcoin's value has risen and fallen rapidly, reaching as much as $19,000 a Bitcoin in December 2017 until plummeting to about $7,000 in the subsequent months. As a result, certain economists regard cryptocurrency as a passing fad or speculation bubble. There is fear because cryptocurrencies such as Bitcoin are not backed by some tangible assets.

According to some studies, the expense of manufacturing a Bitcoin, which consumes a growing amount of electricity, is closely linked to its stock price. While cryptocurrency Blockchains are extremely stable, other elements of the cryptocurrency environment, such as exchanges and wallets, are vulnerable to hacking.

Several internet platforms have been hacked and robbed during Bitcoin's ten-year period, with millions of dollars in "coins" stolen in some cases. Despite this, many analysts see cryptocurrencies as having possible benefits, such as the ability to preserve value against inflation and facilitate trade while being simpler to transfer and divide than valuable stones and operating beyond the reach of central banks and governments.

Chapter 3: Blockchain: Limitations, Misconceptions, and Hacking

We don't believe anybody anticipated the impact of Bitcoin, a Peer-to-Peer Cryptography Mailing List, which was launched in 2008 and presented as a solely peer-to-peer version of digital money. Blockchain and Bitcoin, the network it ran on, was created by the unknown Satoshi Nakamoto and have since grown to become one of the world's most important and groundbreaking innovations.

From banking to engineering to schooling, this technology has the potential to affect and shape any sector. This is how we arrived. Bitcoin was introduced to the open-source world shortly after the whitepaper was released in early 2009, and it was able to address a number of issues related to digital trust by allowing users to archive sensitive details freely without the possibility of it being interfered with.

It's completely open, time-stamped, decentralized, and fraud-proof. Many people now believe that Bitcoin and Blockchain are the same things, and they're not.

parseDouble

What Makes a Blockchain Withstand Hacks?

It's almost difficult to "hack" a Blockchain. But what makes decentralized ledgers so "unhackable" in the first place? The hacking of a Blockchain is sometimes confused with the hacking of a digital exchange, which is a frequent error made by new cryptocurrency investors. Although centralized digital trades are sadly compromised more often than they should be, decentralized Blockchain attacks are very uncommon because they are difficult to achieve and have little opportunity to carry out.

A little History

By 2014, several people had realized that the Blockchain could be used for a wide range of tasks. It provided an incredibly efficient mechanism that could greatly reduce the expense of a variety of transactions as a decentralized, distributed ledger that can document transactions between two individuals in a permanent manner without any need for third-party authentication.

As the promise of the technology was realized, there was a surge of spending and research into how it could be used to streamline procedures of supply chains, banking, hospitals, shipping and infrastructure, voting, and even contract management. About 18% of financial companies are currently utilizing Blockchain technologies in their operations in 2018, and this figure is expected to skyrocket.

To guarantee that every deal is completed correctly, we must either appoint a third agent, draft a contract, or place our confidence in the other party concerned. None of these solutions are foolproof because we can't trust outsiders. Drafting a contract requires time and resources, and having a designated third party can be expensive and time-consuming as well.

This Is Where the Blockchain Comes in

The Blockchain is the ideal solution since it provides a fourth alternative that is safe, simple, and cost-effective. You may compose a few lines of code that would enable the payment to be released to the other party until those requirements are fulfilled.

It works in a similar way to an electronic signature, but it is implemented entirely on the Blockchain without any of the requirements for any external instructions, behavior, or intervention. It works as a collection of digital data, each of which constitutes a financial register entry or a record of a single transaction. Each payment is electronically stamped and validated to guarantee that it is genuine and that it has not been tampered with.

The ledger and the transactions on it have a strong level of trustworthiness. The very interesting part is that these public ledger entries are spread around the Blockchain networks, which ensures that these extra nodes or layers have a consensus mechanism that contains transparency on the status of a transaction at every second and recreates all the signed ledgers that are then dispersed among them.

Whenever a new payment is initiated, a plurality of the node in the Blockchain application is required to run an algorithm that examines and validates the background of the proposed Blockchain block. A new block of transactions is admitted into the database, and a new block is attached to the chain of transactions if the majority of the nodes believe that the signature and history are correct.

If the plurality does not agree that the latest transaction can be attached to the chain, it is rejected and not added. This model enables the Blockchain to function as a public ledger without the need for a centralized, unifying body to determine what is and is not legitimate.

Decentralized and Open-Source Protocols

Many cryptocurrencies' Blockchains are peer-to-peer (P2P), open-source, and accessible, enabling anybody with the right equipment and expertise to see within. This is critical for promoting openness and attracting consumers. A Blockchain is a set of computational processes that operate collectively to achieve a shared purpose.

Proof of-Stake and Proof-of-Work, for example, are consensus structures that secure the network by detecting security from hackers. The decentralized existence of a Blockchain ensures that its network is spread through several computers called nodes. This removes the possibility of a single point of failure.

To put it another way, you can't "cut the head off the serpent" when there isn't one. A Blockchain's design specifies how nodes collaborate to validate a transaction until it is assigned to the protocol. Before a trade may be committed in Bitcoin and other PoW schemes, including Bitcoin Cash, a minimum of 51% of the nodes must consent to it.

Hashing Algorithm

Each transfer is referred to as a block, and the chain of transactions is referred to as a Blockchain. A block is distinguished by cryptographic components that render it one-of-a-kind. The hashing algorithm of a network decides the specifics.

The Bitcoin Blockchain, for example, employs a double SHA-256 hash algorithm, which converts transaction data into a 256-bit hash. A contract becomes rigid by finding it difficult to undo the hashed value.

Every block in a chain comprises a subset of the previous block's results. As a consequence, and though a malicious attacker offsets the hash, the resulting block will be out of line with the rest of the blocks because the hash performance will be different, forcing the machine to refuse it.

Blockchain Fundamentals

51% Attacks Are Improbable

Thanks to its growing hash capacity, the further a Blockchain persists and the more users it receives, the less probable it is to experience a 51% attack. Notice that a hacker has to manipulate at least 51% of a Blockchain's capacity to reconfigure a transaction's hash.

At any stage, this becomes incredibly expensive. As a result, given the scale of existing Blockchains such as Bitcoin and Ethereum, such a situation is almost difficult to imagine.

What About Quantum Computing?

Another explanation that a Blockchain is more difficult to compromise is that if the re-hashed block is in the center of the chain, the intruder will have to re-hash past blocks to match their traditional stamp with the current block.

This is only possible for Bitcoin with the next iteration of quantum computing, which does not yet exist. And even if it does, who's to say that a Blockchain-based quantum defense mechanism won't be developed to counter quantum attacks?

PoS-Based Hacks

Stakes assess the network's power in PoS-based networks. To clarify, this refers to consumers who have delegated or deliberately locked their indigenous Blockchain properties so that they can engage in transparency and traceability and block discovery.

When a hacker holds a plurality of the stake in such a scheme, an assault happens. If a hacker obtains more than 51% of all currency in circulation, anything is likely. This is almost unlikely for respectable networks like the Ethereum 2.0 Blockchain, which is also emerging. Imagine having to raise the money to purchase 51% of Ethereum's estimated market cap of $68 billion.

Economics of a 51%

You won't be able to carry out a covert 51% attack without causing so much scarcity since your purchases would cause the valuation of the remaining coins to spike.

Once Blockchain participants learn that you own the bulk of the tokens, they would undoubtedly sell their shares, causing the price to collapse due to excess supply. As a result, you'll find yourself purchasing big and selling low.

Hash Rate

That is an excellent issue. It all comes down to network power. Bitcoin Gold, Ethereum Classic, Electroneum, and, most recently, Grin have all been casualties of the 51% attack.

The PoW consensus algorithm is used on the Ethereum Classic network. About the fact that ETC uses the very same algorithm as Bitcoin, it has a far smaller number of miners and nodes to keep the device safe.

As a result, the computing capacity is reduced, making it possible for an intruder to gain access. ETC possesses the hash rate of 1.6 tera hashes per second, compared to 117.9 exa hashes per second for Bitcoin.

The Future of Blockchain Hacks

Nobody has ever compromised a Blockchain of their own. Instead, a community of cybercriminals or the core design teams typically work together to compromise a Blockchain's protection.

However, when Blockchain networks get more powerful as a result of the addition of more nodes or stakers, the likelihood of a decentralized network being hacked decreases. Furthermore, newer Blockchain technologies use academically validated approaches that will necessitate the use of extremely advanced quantum computers to decrypt.

To summarize, you now have the means to (politely) correct anyone who claims that a "Blockchain was stolen" and send them on their way.

Who Own the Blockchain?

You've already read a lot about Blockchain technology. It's all over the place. We have just scratched the surface of its success in terms of revolutionizing the way we do things, from conducting financial transfers to handling documents and contracts. The response is that no one really owns Blockchain technology, while separate organizations can own unique and individual Blockchains.

It's important to note that Blockchain and Blockchain technology are not the same thing. Technology is the philosophy and theory that underpins the function of a Blockchain, and it can be repeated and utilized by anybody who wants to. In other words, it is the mechanism or theory that governs its implementation and execution.

Although Satoshi Nakamoto is mostly synonymous with Blockchain technology, the technology and ideas that underpin it are far older than the Blockchain's creation in 2008. W. Stuart Haber and Stuart Haber teamed up in 1991 to establish W. Stuart Haber and W. Stuart Haber. Scott Stornetta spoke about some work he and his colleagues were doing on a cryptographically protected chain of blocks that enabled several documents to be compiled into a single block.

But it doesn't matter who comes up with the first concept for Blockchain technology because it's just a framework, and protocols are used in correspondence in the same manner as programming languages are used in computations.

- Much like you can't assert ownership of C++ or JavaScript, you can't claim ownership of Blockchain technologies either.
- Although most people believe that you cannot assert possession of a programming language, you may claim ownership of an application created for that language.

Many businesses are creating their own private Blockchains and thereby become operators of the technology. However, possessing a ledger is not the same as owning Blockchain technologies.

Blockchain 2.0 is an advanced programming language that makes it possible to create smart contracts, such as invoices that compensate themselves or share certificates that will simply give their owners dividends when profits exceed a certain amount.

But Who Owns the Blockchain?

Our money is stored in a vault, our internet is delivered by a service company, our transfers are processed by a third party, and anything needs slogging up, signing in, or approval.

But Not with the Blockchain

It's difficult to get our minds around the idea that the Blockchain isn't regulated or operated by someone person, but we aim to clarify how it functions in greater depth.

Conclusion

While Bitcoin's revolutionary potential has already been demonstrated through the rapid emergence of a community of users and broad market diversity, few people emphasize the real power behind cryptocurrencies: Blockchain technology.

Blockchains will do for networks and business ecosystems what enterprise resource planning (ERP) did for the individual enterprise.

The Blockchain can be said to represent a ledger; it keeps track of all transactions made in the system in chronological order and ensures the cohesion and consistency of the account status of all users. The particularity of this structure is that it does not exist anywhere, but is distributed throughout the network. In addition, it has a fairly robust verification protocol, so robust as to be able to program economies and decentralized communication protocols, secure, and also open source. Bitcoin, in particular, takes advantage of these features to implement its digital currency.

The fact that the code of all these systems is open, not only allows anyone to develop their own cryptocurrencies (approximately 530 as of this date, according to Wikipedia), but it is also possible to modify the protocol and create secure and decentralized computing systems for many other use cases.

Let's imagine that now in the Blockchain we do not only store monetary statements, but programs. Or that it is no longer just currencies, but contracts or any other type of document, even operating systems. This makes it possible to implement complex "worlds," networks within the network, with their own economies and rules. All this in a strongly protected environment, and where the computing power of the entire network can be harnessed, due to its distributed nature.

9 781801 565011